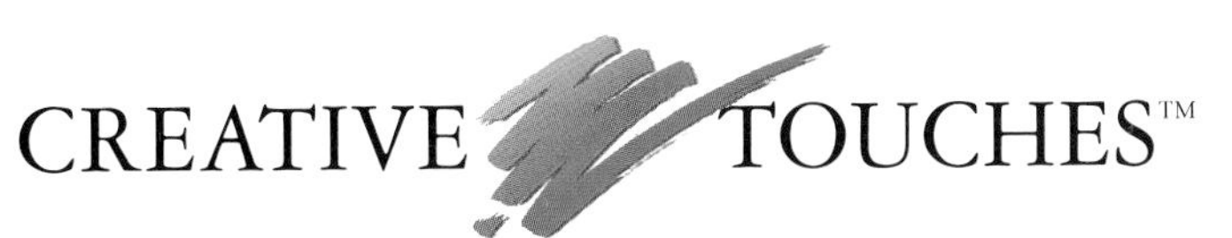

ETC.

THE HOME DECORATING INSTITUTE®

Library of Congress Cataloging-in-Publication Data Metallic finishes etc. p. cm. — (Creative touches)
Includes index. ISBN 0-86573-875-0 (softcover) 1. Texture painting. 2. Gilding. 3. Interior decoration. I. Cy DeCosse Incorporated. II. Series.
TT323.M47 1996 745.7'2—dc20 96-28583

Contents

Getting Started

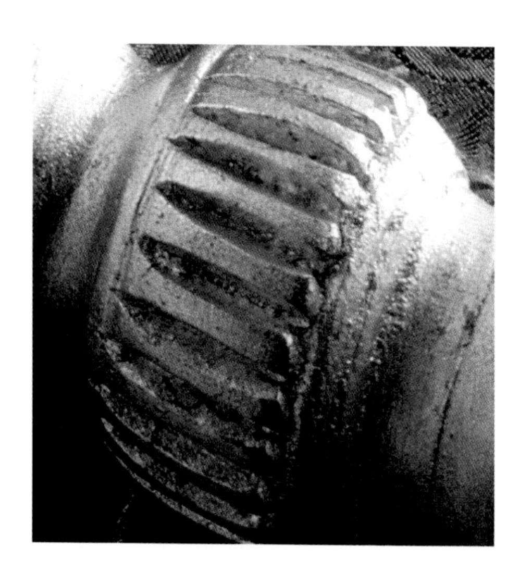

Painted Metallic Finishes

Gilded Finishes

Metallic Finishes ETC.

The luster of a metallic finish can create an aura of extravagance and luxury. Though rich in appearance, metallic finishes can be achieved through a variety of inexpensive techniques.

Faux metallic finishes can be created with paint, often in combination with other substances, to create textured effects. These include aged metallic finishes, such as rust and verdigris. An elegant wall treatment is achieved with metallic acrylic paints in a technique called scumbling. Even spray paints can be used in a unique manner to create a metallic marbleized effect on small items, such as picture frames.

Authentic metallic effects are produced by applying metal leaf or metallic powders to a surface, in processes known as gilding. Using a variety of methods, the metal-leafed surface can be given an old-world, antique charm. Furniture or accent pieces can be embellished with gleaming metallic stenciled designs.

The ideas and techniques taught in this book will inspire you to add creative metallic touches throughout your home. With beautiful photography and expert instructions as your guide, learning is the fun part.

GETTING STARTED

Primers & Finishes

PRIMERS

Some surfaces must be coated with a primer before the paint is applied. Primers ensure good adhesion of paint and are used to seal porous surfaces so paint will spread smoothly without soaking in. It is usually not necessary to prime a nonporous surface in good condition, such as smooth, unchipped, previously painted wood or wallboard. Many types of water-based primers are available; select one that is suitable for the type of surface you are painting.

A. FLAT LATEX PRIMER is used for sealing unfinished wallboard. It makes the surface nonporous so fewer coats of paint are needed. This primer may also be used to seal previously painted wallboard before you apply new paint of a dramatically different color. The primer prevents the original color from showing through.

B. LATEX ENAMEL UNDERCOAT is used for priming most raw woods or woods that have been previously painted or stained. A wood primer closes the pores of the wood, for a smooth surface. It is not used for cedar, redwood, or plywoods that contain water-soluble dyes, because the dyes would bleed through the primer.

C. RUST-INHIBITING LATEX METAL PRIMER helps paint adhere to metal. Once a rust-inhibiting primer is applied, water-based paint may be used on metal without causing the surface to rust.

D. POLYVINYL ACRYLIC PRIMER, or PVA, is used to seal the porous surface of plaster and unglazed pottery, if a smooth paint finish is desired. To preserve the texture of plaster or unglazed pottery, apply the paint directly to the surface without using a primer.

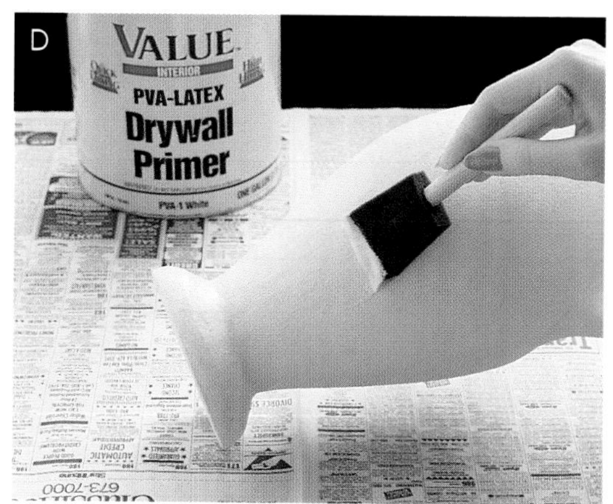

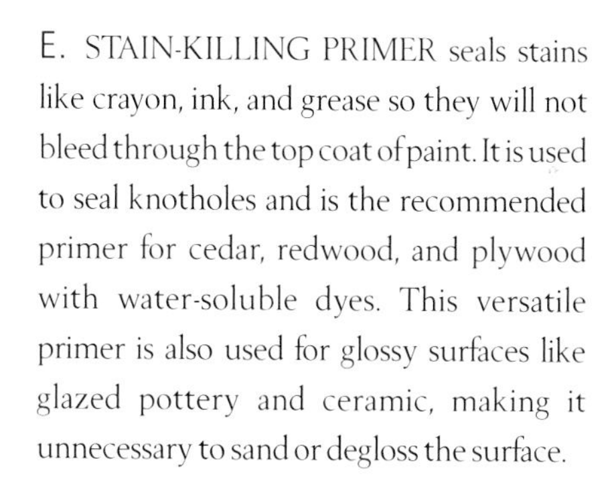

E. STAIN-KILLING PRIMER seals stains like crayon, ink, and grease so they will not bleed through the top coat of paint. It is used to seal knotholes and is the recommended primer for cedar, redwood, and plywood with water-soluble dyes. This versatile primer is also used for glossy surfaces like glazed pottery and ceramic, making it unnecessary to sand or degloss the surface.

FINISHES

Finishes are sometimes used over paint as the final coat. They protect the painted surface with a transparent coating. The degree of protection and durability varies, from a light application of matte aerosol sealer to a glossy layer of clear finish.

F. CLEAR FINISH, such as water-based urethanes and acrylics, may be used over painted finishes for added durability. Available in matte, satin, and gloss, these clear finishes are applied with a brush or sponge applicator. Environmentally safe clear finishes are available in pints, quarts, and gallons (0.5, 0.9, and 3.8 L) at paint supply stores and in 4-oz. and 8-oz. (119 and 237 mL) bottles or jars at craft stores.

G. AEROSOL CLEAR ACRYLIC SEALER, available in matte or gloss, may be used as the final coat over paint as a protective finish. A gloss sealer also adds sheen and depth to the painted finish for a more polished look. Apply aerosol sealer in several light coats rather than one heavy coat, to avoid dripping or puddling. To protect the environment, select an aerosol sealer that does not contain harmful propellants. Use all sealers in a well-ventilated area.

Tools & Supplies

TAPES

When painting, use tape to mask off any surrounding areas. Several brands are available, varying in the amount of tack, how well they release from the surface without damaging the base coat, and how long they can remain in place before removal. You may want to test the tape before applying it to the entire project. The edge of the tape should be sealed tightly to prevent seepage.

PAINT ROLLERS

Paint rollers are used to paint an area quickly with an even coat of paint. Roller pads, available in several nap thicknesses, are used in conjunction with roller frames. Use synthetic or lamb's wool roller pads to apply water-based paints.

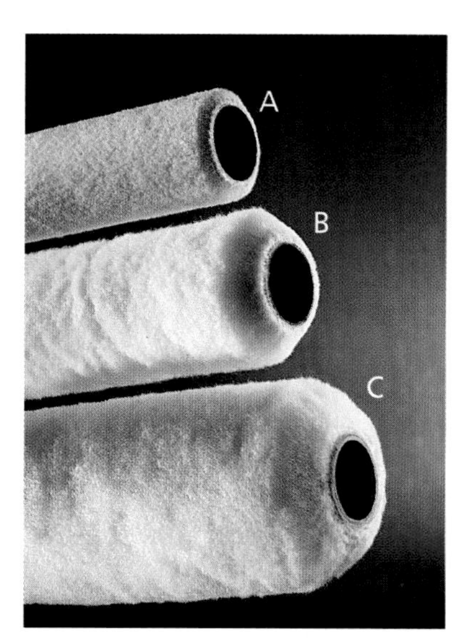

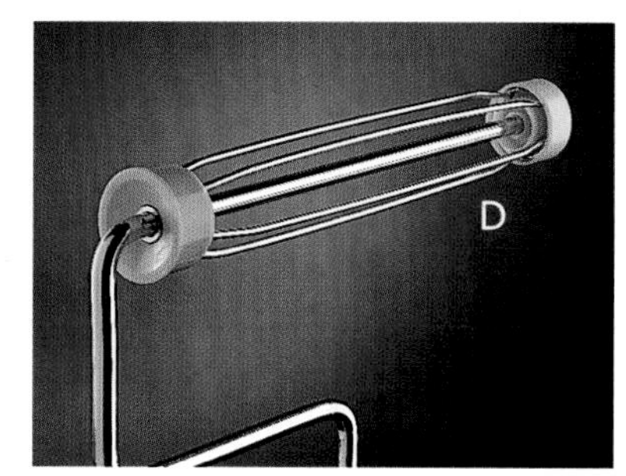

A. SHORT-NAP ROLLER PADS with 1/4" to 3/8" (6 mm to 1 cm) nap are used for applying glossy paints to smooth surfaces like wallboard, wood, and smooth plaster.

B. MEDIUM-NAP ROLLER PADS with 1/2" to 3/4" (1.3 to 2 cm) nap are used as all-purpose pads. They give flat surfaces a slight texture.

C. LONG-NAP ROLLER PADS with 1" to 1 1/4" (2.5 to 3.2 cm) nap are used to cover textured areas in fewer passes.

D. ROLLER FRAME is the metal arm and handle that holds the roller pad in place. A wire cage supports the pad in the middle. Select a roller frame with nylon bearings so it will roll smoothly and a threaded end on the handle so you can attach an extension pole.

E. EXTENSION POLE has a threaded end that screws into the handle of a roller frame. Use an extension pole when painting ceilings, high wall areas, and floors.

E

PAINTBRUSHES & APPLICATORS

Several types of paintbrushes and applicators are available, designed for various purposes. Select the correct one to achieve the best quality in the paint finish.

A. SYNTHETIC-BRISTLE paintbrushes are generally used with water-based latex and acrylic paints, while B. NATURAL-BRISTLE brushes are used with alkyd, or oil-based paints. Natural-bristle paintbrushes may be used with water-based paints to create certain decorative effects.

C. BRUSH COMBS remove dried or stubborn paint particles from paintbrushes and align the bristles so they dry properly. To use a brush comb, hold the brush in a stream of water as you pull the comb several times through the bristles from the base to the tips. Use mild soap on the brush, if necessary, and rinse well. The curved side of the tool can be used to remove paint from the roller pad.

Stencil brushes are available in a range of sizes. Use the small brushes for fine detail work in small stencil openings, and the large brushes for larger openings. Either D. SNYTHETIC or E. NATURAL-BRISTLE stencil brushes may be used with acrylic paints.

Artist's brushes are available in several types, including F. FAN, G. LINER, and H. FLAT BRUSHES. After cleaning the brushes, always reshape the head of the brush by stroking the bristles with your fingers. Store artist's brushes upright on their handles or lying flat so there is no pressure on the bristles.

I. SPONGE APPLICATORS are used for a smooth application of paint on flat surfaces.

J. PAINT EDGERS with guide wheels are used to apply paint next to moldings, ceilings, and corners. The guide wheels can be adjusted for proper alignment of the paint pad.

Preparing the Surface

To achieve a high-quality and long-lasting paint finish that adheres well to the surface, it is important to prepare the surface properly so it is clean and smooth. The preparation steps vary, depending on the type of surface you are painting. Often it is necessary to apply a primer to the surface before painting it. For more information about primers, refer to pages 8 and 9.

PREPARING SURFACES FOR PAINTING

SURFACE TO BE PAINTED	PREPARATION STEPS	PRIMER
UNFINISHED WOOD	1. Sand surface to smooth it. 2. Wipe with damp cloth to remove grit. 3. Apply primer.	Latex enamel undercoat.
PREVIOUSLY PAINTED WOOD	1. Clean surface to remove any grease and dirt. 2. Rinse with clear water; allow to dry. 3. Sand surface lightly to degloss and smooth it and to remove any loose paint chips. 4. Wipe with damp cloth to remove grit. 5. Apply primer to any areas of bare wood.	Not necessary, except to touch up areas of bare wood; then use latex enamel undercoat.
PREVIOUSLY VARNISHED WOOD	1. Clean surface to remove any grease and dirt. 2. Rinse with clear water; allow to dry. 3. Sand surface to degloss it. 4. Wipe with damp cloth to remove grit. 5. Apply primer.	Latex enamel undercoat.
UNFINSHED WALLBOARD	1. Dust with hand broom, or vacuum with soft brush attachment. 2. Apply primer.	Flat latex primer.
PREVIOUSLY PAINTED WALLBOARD	1. Clean surface to remove any grease and dirt. 2. Rinse with clear water; allow to dry. 3. Apply primer, only if making a dramatic color change.	Not necessary, except when painting over dark or strong color; then use flat latex primer.
UNPAINTED PLASTER	1. Sand any flat surfaces as necessary. 2. Dust with hand broom, or vacuum with soft brush attachment.	Polyvinyl acrylic primer.
PREVIOUSLY PAINTED PLASTER	1. Clean surface to remove any grease and dirt. 2. Rinse with clear water; allow to dry thoroughly. 3. Fill any cracks with spackling compound. 4. Sand surface to degloss it.	Not necessary, except when painting over dark or strong color; then use polyvinyl acrylic primer.
UNGLAZED POTTERY	1. Dust with brush, or vacuum with soft brush attachment. 2. Apply primer.	Polyvinyl acrylic primer or gesso.
GLAZED POTTERY, CERAMIC & GLASS	1. Clean surface to remove any grease and dirt. 2. Rinse with clear water; allow to dry thoroughly. 3. Apply primer.	Stain-killing primer.
METAL	1. Clean surface with vinegar or lacquer thinner to remove any grease and dirt. 2. Sand surface to degloss it and to remove any rust. 3. Wipe with damp cloth to remove grit. 4. Apply primer.	Rust-inhibiting latex metal primer.
FABRIC	1. Prewash fabric without fabric softener to remove any sizing, if fabric is washable. 2. Press fabric as necessary.	None.

Paints

A wide variety of paint is available from paint supply stores and craft stores. Each type has advantages that make it especially suitable for certain kinds of painting. Latex and acrylic paints are water-based, making cleanup easy with soap and water. Water-based paints are also safer for the environment than oil-based paints.

LATEX PAINTS

Latex paint is fast drying and durable. In addition to the wide range of premixed colors, latex paint can be custom-mixed by a paint professional. It is available in various finishes, from flat latex for a matte appearance to high-gloss latex with maximum sheen. Low-luster latex enamel paint, sometimes referred to as eggshell enamel, has some sheen and provides good coverage; semigloss has a bit more sheen. The glossier the paint, the more durable it is. Packaged in pints, quarts, and gallons (0.5, 0.9, and 3.8 L), latex paint is suitable for general use in small and large jobs.

Latex paint contains acrylic or vinyl resins or a combination of both. Latex paints of acrylic resins are the highest quality, with vinyl-acrylic blends next in quality, followed by paints consisting solely of vinyl resins. High-quality paints may cost significantly more, but they provide an even, complete coverage and wear longer.

CRAFT ACRYLIC PAINT

Craft acrylic paint contains 100 percent acrylic resins. Generally sold in 2-oz., 4-oz., and 8-oz. (59, 119, and 237 mL) bottles or jars, these premixed acrylics have a creamy brushing consistency and give excellent coverage. They should not be confused with the thicker artist's acrylics used for canvas paintings. Craft acrylic paint can be diluted with water, acrylic extender, or latex paint conditioner if a thinner consistency is desired. Craft acrylic paints are available in many colors and in metallic, fluorescent, and iridescent formulas.

OIL-BASED PAINTS

Oil-based paints are available in both aerosol and brush-on forms. Use them only when water-based paints cannot be used to achieve the desired effect, since they are more harmful to the environment and more difficult to clean up than water-based paints. They have a longer drying time and are available in a variety of colors, including many metallics. Always use oil-based paints in well-ventilated areas and avoid inhaling the fumes.

PAINTED METALLIC FINISHES

Faux Verdigris

Faux verdigris is an easy paint finish that has the aged look of tarnished copper, brass, or bronze. Intended for indoor use, faux verdigris works well on cement or plaster statues, and on clay pots with relief designs, for a look as realistic as verdigris pieces of sculpted metal.

To simulate the irregular, weathered appearance of aged metals, a bright aqua paint is applied randomly over a base coat of black or metallic paint. Then a paste made from concrete patching materials and paint is applied, to give added texture and color variation.

In the early stages of verdigris, the aging appears in the recessed areas while the raised areas remain metallic. In faux verdigris, this look is accomplished by using a metallic base coat.

In the advanced stage of verdigris, the recesses have become blackened with age and the raised areas have a weathered appearance due to greenish blue deposits. This look is achieved in faux verdigris by starting with a black base coat.

MATERIALS

- Flat latex or craft acrylic paint in black or metallic, for the base coat.
- Flat latex or craft acrylic paints in bright aqua and white.
- Dry concrete patch and concrete adhesive, available at hardware stores and builder's supply stores.
- Synthetic paintbrushes.
- Toothbrush.
- Disposable plate and cup.
- Spray bottle, such as a plant sprayer.

VERDIGRIS PASTE

Mix together the following ingredients:

One part bright aqua latex or craft acrylic paint.

Six parts white latex or craft acrylic paint.

Twelve parts dry concrete patch.

Two parts concrete adhesive.

How to apply a faux verdigris finish

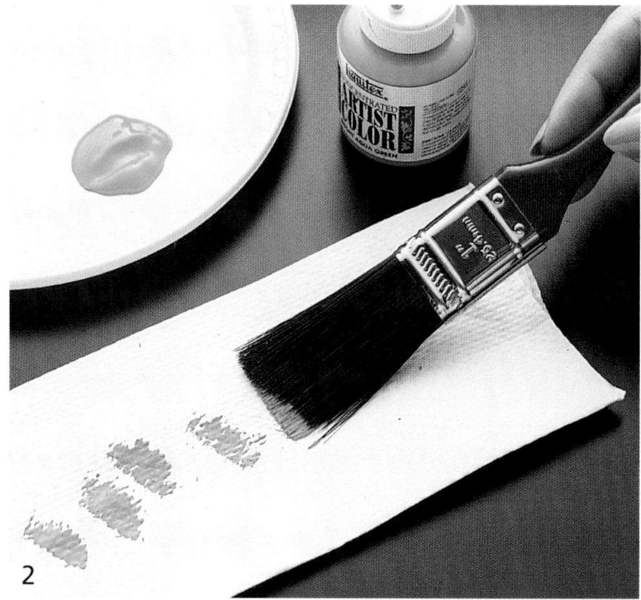

1. Apply an even base coat of black or metallic paint to clean surface, using synthetic paintbrush, making sure paint is applied into any crevices or recessed areas. Allow paint to dry.

2. Pour small amount of aqua paint onto disposable plate. Thin to a creamy consistency by adding water, if necessary. Dip the tip of the brush into paint; blot on paper towel to remove excess paint.

3. Apply aqua paint randomly with paintbrush in an up-and-down motion called stippling, leaving some base coat exposed. Over black base coat, apply aqua paint to raised areas; over metallic base coat, apply aqua paint to flat or recessed areas.

4. Smear aqua paint in some areas, if desired, using a dry paintbrush.

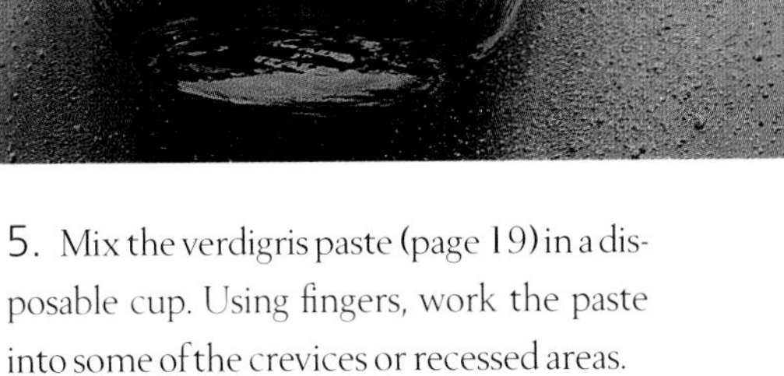

5. Mix the verdigris paste (page 19) in a disposable cup. Using fingers, work the paste into some of the crevices or recessed areas.

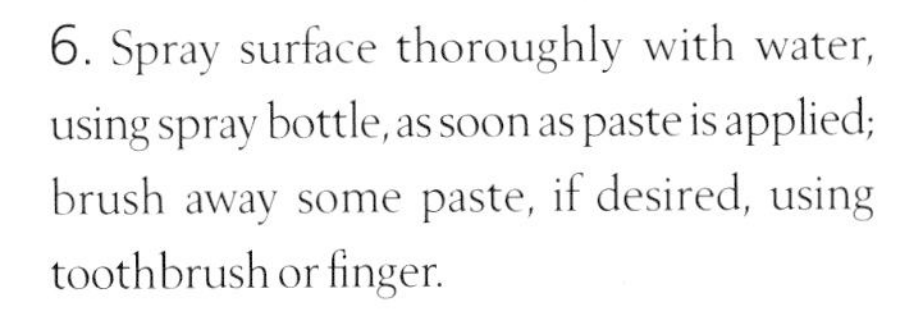

6. Spray surface thoroughly with water, using spray bottle, as soon as paste is applied; brush away some paste, if desired, using toothbrush or finger.

7. Drizzle small amount of dry concrete patch over wet areas. Once dry, concrete cannot be removed.

FOR METALLIC FINISHES ONLY. Reapply the metallic paint as necessary to highlight the raised areas. This gives metallics a realistic verdigris appearance, with the more aged aqua areas in the recesses and the shiny, less weathered finish in the raised areas.

More ideas for faux verdigris

ABOVE: PLASTER, METAL, AND WOODEN ACCESSORIES have faux verdigris finishes with bronze, black, and brass base coats.

OPPOSITE, TOP: METAL SWING-ARM RODS have a faux verdigris finish with a bronze base coat.

OPPOSITE, BOTTOM: FAUX VERDIGRIS FINISH was applied to the raised design area on a brass planter.

Faux Rust

A faux rust finish has a timeworn look that complements country, primitive, and contemporary decorating schemes. Finished in faux rust, accessories like lamp bases, picture frames, boxes, vases, candlesticks, and shelf brackets add warm, rustic charm to interiors.

A paste of concrete patching materials and acrylic paints is applied to the surface over a base coat of black paint. For a realistic rusted appearance, use a natural sea sponge to dab paste onto the surface, letting some of the black base coat show. After the paste has dried, sponge paint a light application of burnt sienna craft acrylic paint over the surface.

For the lighter faux rust finish on the horse (opposite), the amounts of the burnt umber and burnt sienna paints in the rust paste were transposed; and, for the sponge-painted top coat, a small amount of yellow oxide craft acrylic paint was mixed into the burnt sienna.

MATERIALS

- Flat latex or craft acrylic paint in black.
- Craft acrylic paints in burnt sienna and burnt umber.
- Dry concrete patch.
- Concrete adhesive.
- Natural sea sponge.
- Disposable cup or bowl.

RUST PASTE

Mix together the following ingredients:

One part burnt sienna craft acrylic paint.

Six parts burnt umber craft acrylic paint.

Twelve parts dry concrete patch.

Two parts concrete adhesive.

How to apply a faux rust paint finish

1. Apply a base coat of black paint, using a synthetic paintbrush. Allow paint to dry.

2. Mix rust paste (page 25) in disposable cup or bowl. Using a spoon, apply a thin layer of paste onto dampened sea sponge.

3. Smudge the paste onto entire surface, using sponge; allow some of the base coat to show. Then dab with a sea sponge to give a stippled look. Allow to dry.

4. Dip small sea sponge into burnt sienna paint; blot on paper towel. Apply small amount to surface, to brighten rust finish. Allow to dry.

How to apply a simple rust or verdigris finish

To achieve the look of verdigris or rust quickly, a simplified method can be used. The resulting finish does not have the rough texture provided by the concrete patch used in the methods on pages 19 to 26. The colors and visual textures of the finishes do, however, resemble real verdigris and rust.

MATERIALS

- Primer recommended for type of surface; for a metal surface, use a rust-inhibiting latex metal primer.
- Latex or acrylic paint in black, for base coat.
- Latex or acrylic paint in burnt sienna, for rust finish; latex or acrylic paint in aqua, for verdigris finish.
- Sandpaper; tack cloth.
- Paintbrush; natural sea sponge.

1. Clean the surface to remove any grease and dirt. Rinse with clear water; allow to dry. Sand lightly to degloss the surface; wipe with a tack cloth to remove grit. Apply primer; allow to dry.

2. Apply base coat of black paint. Dip small sea sponge into burnt sienna or aqua paint; blot on a paper towel. Apply to the surface in an up-and-down motion, to give a stippled look. Allow to dry.

Antiqued Metallic Finishes

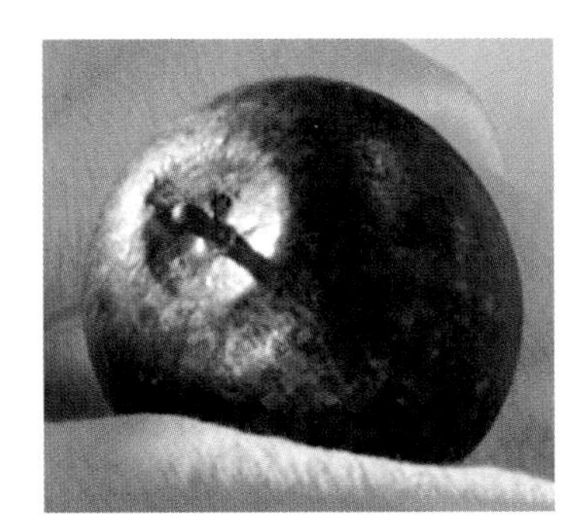

Any surface that can be painted can be given an authentic antiqued metallic finish. Acrylic paints that contain finely ground metal particles, such as those developed by Modern Options, are painted onto a primed surface. Before the paint dries, Modern Options' antiquing solutions are applied; they react with the metal, causing verdigris patinas or rust to form. Copper Topper™, Gilded Gold™, Blackened Bronze Base™, and Blonde Bronze Base™ are acrylic metallic paints that can be antiqued with Patina Green™ and Patina Blue™ antiquing solutions, creating a verdigris finish. Silver Plate™ acrylic metallic paint can be given an antiqued look, using Burgundy Tint™ or Black Tint™ tinting solutions. Instant Iron™ acrylic metallic paint develops a rust when Instant Rust™ antiquing solution is applied.

Since the metal particles tend to sink to the bottom of the bottle, always shake the bottle well before, and several times during, application. Build up the paint base with several thin coats, allowing each to dry thoroughly before the next is applied. Apply antiquing solution to the top coat when it is still wet or tacky, allowing the solution to react with the metal. Once dry, a natural sealant in the paint prevents the solution from reacting with the metal particles, with the exception of Instant Iron, which can be antiqued while wet or dry.

Repeated applications of the antiquing solution will intensify the patina or rust finish. A matte aerosol acrylic sealer will prevent the finish from rubbing off when handled as well as prevent further natural aging of the piece.

Thoroughly read and follow the manufacturer's instructions for use of these products. Wear rubber gloves and goggles, and avoid inhaling the fumes or vapors of the antiquing solutions.

How to apply a copper, brass, or bronze verdigris finish

MATERIALS

- Acrylic metallic paint containing finely ground metal, such as Modern Options' Copper Topper™, Gilded Gold™, Blackened Bronze Base™, or Blonde Bronze Base™.
- Sponge applicator.
- Antiquing solutions, such as Modern Options' Patina Green™ and Patina Blue™.
- Tinting solutions, such as Modern Options' Burgundy Tint™ and Black Tint™, optional.
- Small glass or plastic bowls; disposable applicator, such as stiff-bristled brush, sponge, or cloth rag.
- Matte aerosol clear acrylic sealer.

1. Shake paint thoroughly. Pour small amount into bowl. Apply thin layer to surface, using sponge applicator; allow to dry. Repeat two or three times, until painted surface is fully opaque.

2. Apply thin top coat of paint. Pour small amount of antiquing solution into bowl; apply solution to surface while top coat is still wet or tacky, using desired applicator. Allow solution to react with metallic paint until dry.

3. Apply additional thin coats of the same antiquing solution or second solution, if desired, allowing the surface to dry completely between coats. If more color variation is desired, apply tinting solution in strategic areas; allow to dry.

4. Allow antiqued finish to develop for two or three days. Apply two thin coats of matte aerosol clear acrylic sealer.

How to apply an antiqued silver finish

MATERIALS

- Silver acrylic metallic paint containing finely ground metal, such as Modern Options' Silver Plate™.
- Sponge applicator.
- Tinting solutions, such as Modern Options' Burgundy Tint™ and Black Tint™.
- Small glass or plastic bowls; disposable applicator, such as brush, sponge, or cloth rag.
- Matte aerosol acrylic sealer.

1. Shake paint thoroughly. Pour a small amount into bowl. Apply thin layer to surface, using sponge applicator; allow to dry. Repeat two or three times, until painted surface is fully opaque.

2. Apply thin top coat of paint. Pour small amounts of tinting solutions into separate bowls. Apply solutions to surface while top coat is still wet or tacky, using desired applicators; blend solutions on surface to achieve desired effect. Tinting solutions do not react with paint. Allow to dry.

3. Repeat application of tinting solutions, if desired; allow to dry. Apply two thin coats of matte aerosol clear acrylic sealer.

How to apply a rusted iron finish

MATERIALS

- Acrylic metallic paint containing finely ground iron, such as Modern Options' Instant Iron™.
- Sponge applicator.
- Antiquing solution, such as Modern Options' Instant Rust™.
- Small glass or plastic bowls; disposable applicator, such as stiff-bristled brush, sponge, or cloth rag.
- Matte aerosol clear acrylic sealer.

3

4

1. Shake paint thoroughly. Pour small amount into bowl. Apply thin layer to the surface, using sponge applicator; allow to dry. Repeat two or three times, until painted surface is fully opaque.

2A. ORANGE RUST. Apply thin top coat of paint. Pour small amount of antiquing solution into bowl; apply solution to the surface while top coat is still wet or tacky, using desired applicator. Allow solution to react with metallic paint until dry.

2B. RED-BROWN RUST. Allow paint to cure 24 hours. Pour small amount of antiquing solution into bowl; apply the solution to surface, using desired applicator. Allow solution to react with metallic paint until dry.

3. Apply additional thin coats of antiquing solution if richer rust is desired, allowing the surface to dry completely between coats.

4. Allow rust to develop for three or four days. Apply two thin coats of matte aerosol clear acrylic sealer.

Scumbled Wall Designs

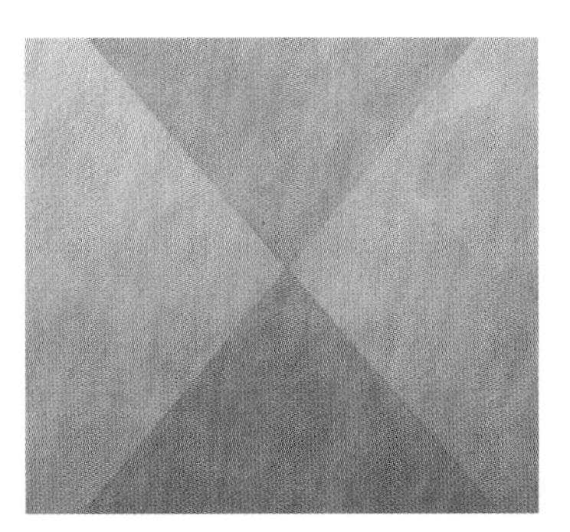

The wall treatment you select makes a significant impact on the total decorating scheme. You can mimic the look of expensive wallcovering, using a painting technique called scumbling to create textural geometric patterns.

In the scumbling technique, a large stencil brush is used to dry-brush paint onto the wall in swirling motions, over a base coat. Because only a minimal amount of paint is required for dry brushing, small jars of acrylic metallic paints can be used. Choose two or three related colors. Or, for a look that is classic and rich, use gold and silver metallic paints.

You can customize the geometric design, covering an entire wall, if desired, as shown for the diamond design, opposite. Or plan a chair rail in a block pattern, a ceiling border made of triangular shapes, or a striped wainscoting, as shown on pages 38 and 39. Use painter's masking tape to mask off the designs.

Measure each wall, and plan the desired design on graph paper to help decide on the scale and placement of the geometric design. Before painting the walls, experiment with the painting technique, making a test sample on a sheet of cardboard.

To prepare the surface, clean the walls, removing any dirt or grease, and rinse them with clear water. If the walls are unfinished, apply a primer and allow it to dry. Then apply the base coat, allowing it to dry thoroughly before the masking tape is applied.

MATERIALS

- Painter's masking tape.
- Wide-blade putty knife.
- Carpenter's level; straightedge.
- Latex paint, for base coat.
- Acrylic metallic paints in desired colors, for scumbling.
- Stencil brush, 1" (2.5 cm) in diameter.
- Disposable plate; paper towels.

How to paint a scumbled wall design

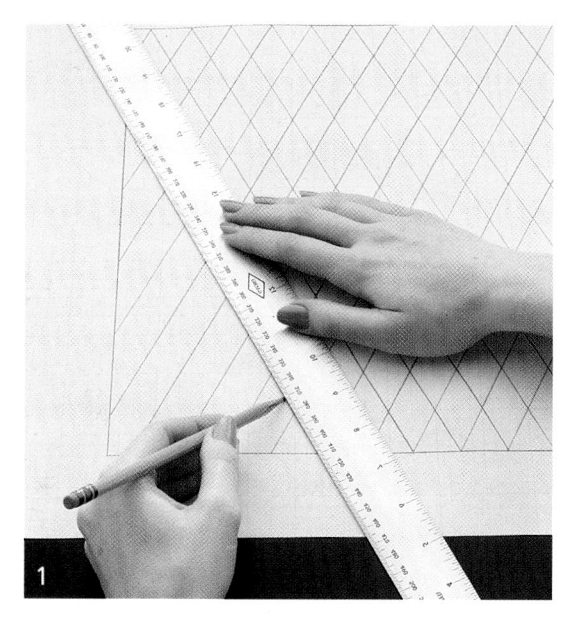
1

2

1. Measure the wall. Plan the design to scale on graph paper.

2. Apply base coat of paint, using paint roller; allow to dry thoroughly. Draw design on wall in light pencil markings, using carpenter's level and straightedge.

3. Indicate which areas are to be masked off, using small pieces of masking tape. Apply painter's masking tape to marked areas; use a putty knife to trim the masking tape diagonally at corners as shown. Press firmly along all edges of tape, using plastic credit card or your fingernail to seal tightly.

4. Pour a small amount of each paint color onto disposable plate. Dip the tip of the stencil brush into first color. Using a circular motion, blot brush onto folded paper towel until the bristles are almost dry.

3

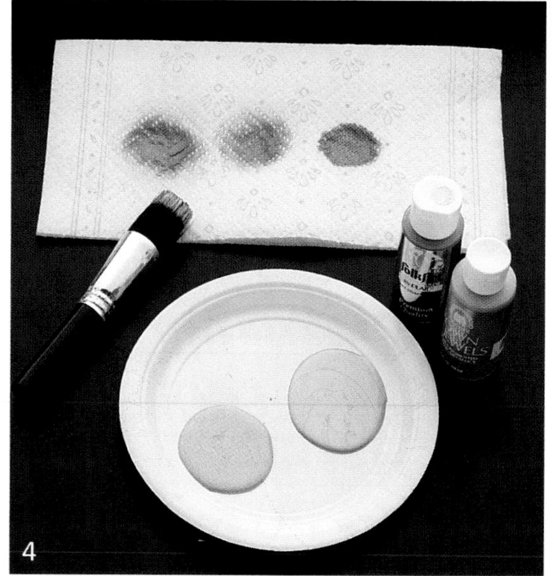
4

5

6

5. Wrap fingers around handle of brush as if to make a fist. Brush paint onto the wall in vigorous, wide, circular motions, working in a small area at a time and changing the direction of the circular motions frequently; overlap the paint onto the masking tape. Build up the color to desired intensity, but allow base coat to show through. Use all of the paint on bristles.

6. Dip the stencil brush into the second color; blot. Apply the paint randomly over the same area, building up color to varying intensities throughout the area. Repeat with a third color, if desired.

7. Repeat the technique to complete the entire wall, working in one small area at a time and blending areas together. Remove masking tape when paint is dry.

7

More ideas for scumbled wall designs

TOP: BORDER DESIGN is composed of triangular shapes. The designs are scumbled, alternating the colors from one triangle to the next.

ABOVE: CHAIR RAIL in a block design adds simple detailing to painted walls.

OPPOSITE, CENTER: OVERALL WALL DESIGN of diamonds within diamonds is created using wide masking tape.

OPPOSITE, BOTTOM: WAINSCOTING features interrupted stripes, scumbled in greens and tans.

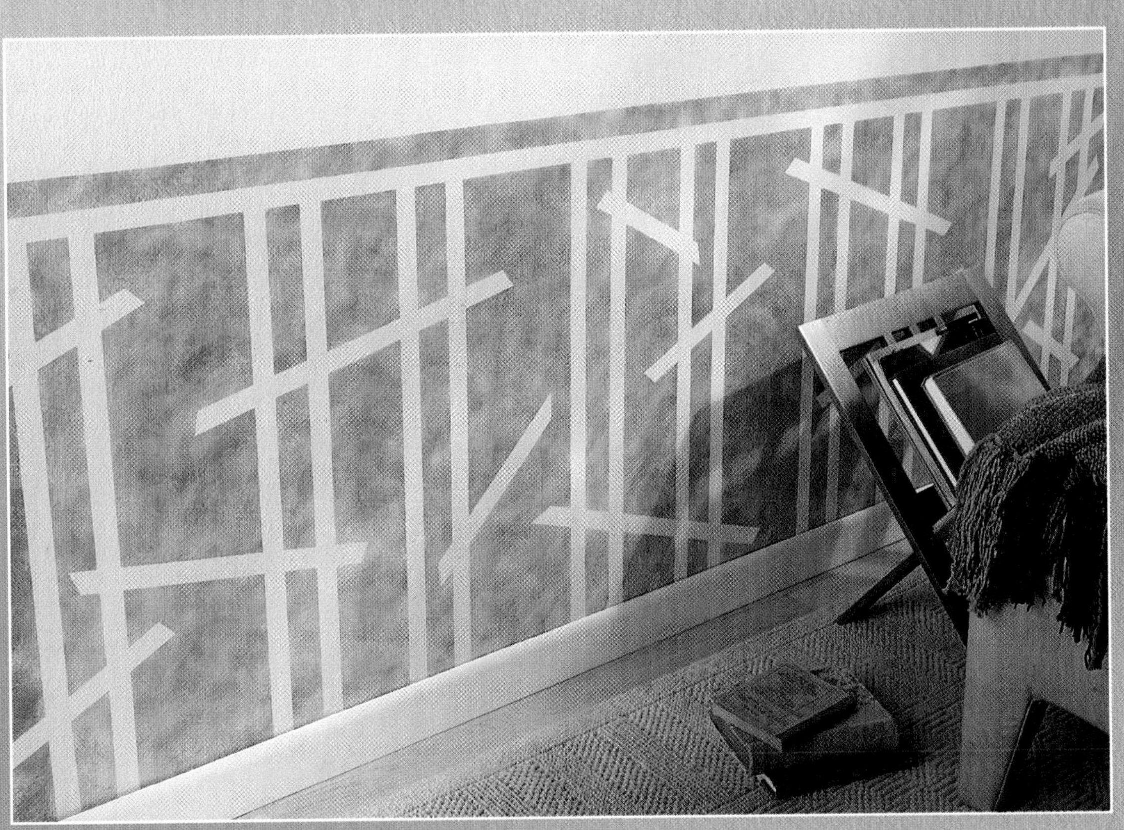

Metallic Marbleizing

The subtle and elegant colors of these marbleized frames are easy to produce, using aerosol enamel and metallic paints. Paint is floated in water; then the frame is dipped into the water to pick up the color randomly. The process can be repeated with multiple colors to produce a mottled, textural effect. This technique can be used on any paintable flat-surfaced or dimensional accessory.

MATERIALS

- Picture frame or other small paintable accessory.
- Oil-based aerosol enamel and metallic paints, for base coat and marbleizing.
- Shallow pan, larger than frame or accessory, such as a disposable aluminum pan.
- Disposable rubber gloves.

How to apply a metallic marbleized finish

1. Apply base coat to the frame in desired color; allow to dry. Pour water into pan to a depth of about 1" (2.5 cm). Spray paint over surface of water.

2. Dip face side of frame into water to coat front and sides with paint; take care to hold frame parallel to surface of water. Remove frame immediately.

3. Skim surface of water with piece of folded newspaper to remove excess paint. Repeat marbleizing process as desired for any remaining paint colors.

1

2
3

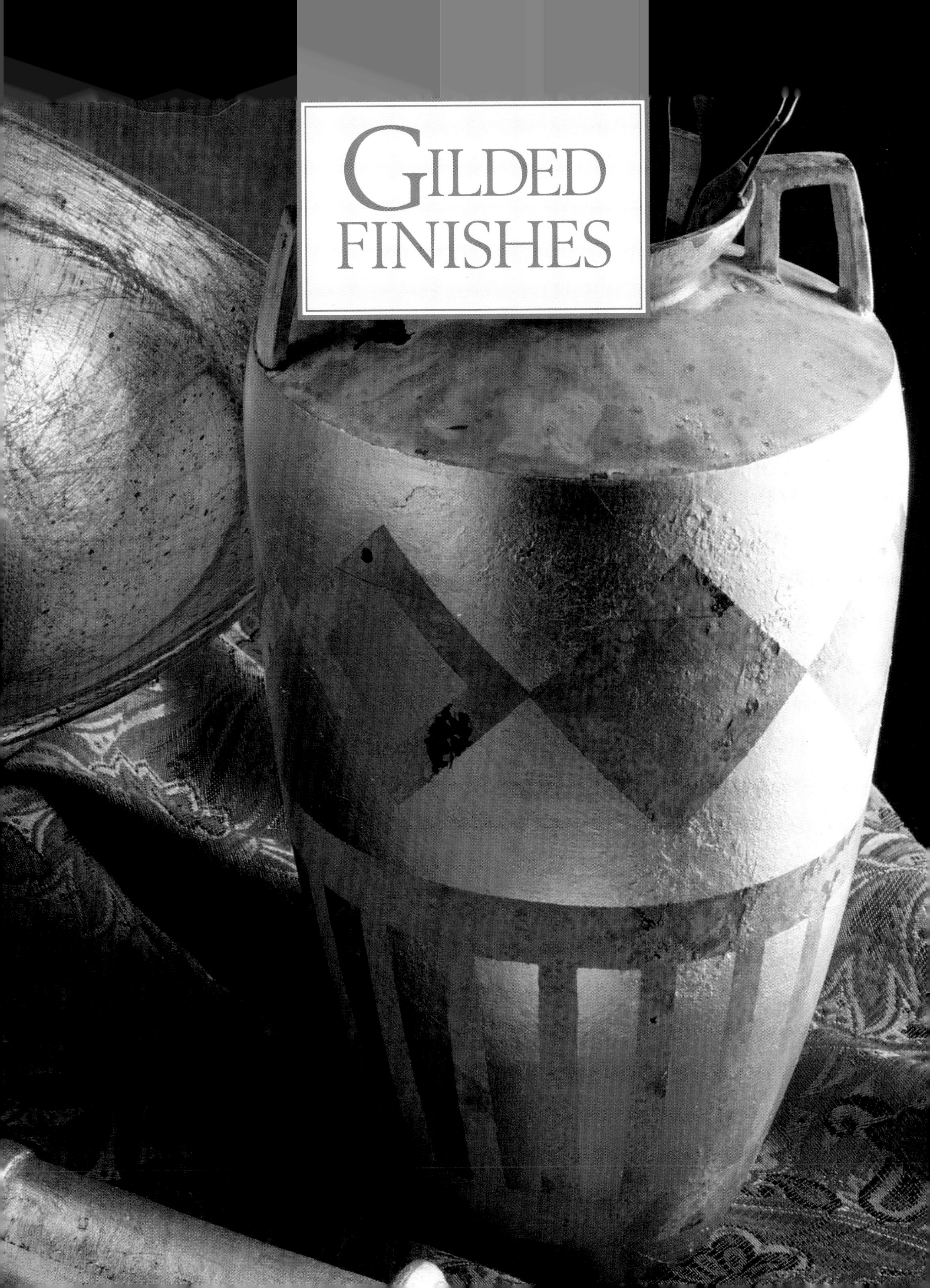

GILDED FINISHES

Metal-leaf Finishes

The ancient craft of metal leafing, or gilding, is used to add elegance and sophistication to furniture and accessories. Tissue-thin sheets of precious or common metals are affixed to a carefully prepared surface, using a special adhesive size, to create a lustrous metallic finish. Pure gold and silver leaf are quite expensive and require very delicate handling. However, composition leaves, made of common metals, mimic gold and silver very successfully and are available at less cost. Composition gold leaf, also known as Dutch metal, is a zinc and copper alloy, while composition silver leaf is actually made of aluminum. Pure copper leaf is also available.

Small accessories may be covered entirely in metal leaf for a bright, bold appearance. When used in isolated areas on furniture or accessories as inlaid or stenciled designs, metal leafing provides a glimmering accent. For a mellow, aged appearance, the metal-leaf finish can be antiqued, using chemical antiquing and tinting solutions (page 49).

Careful preparation of the surface is essential for successful metal leafing. The surface must be as smooth as possible; any irregularities, rough spots, or brush strokes will be amplified by the glossy metal leaf. The base-coat color will affect the color of the slightly translucent metal leaf. A red base coat adds a warm glow when used under gold leaf. A deep green base coat gives copper leaf vibrance, whether left clear and shiny or given an antiqued finish. Black may be used as a base coat under any type of metal leaf but is especially appropriate under silver.

Metal leaf is purchased in books of twenty-five leaves, each measuring 5 1/2" × 5 1/2" (14 × 14 cm). The leaves are separated by sheets of tissue paper, which must be used when handling the leaf, to prevent fingerprints from marring the metal. Thin cotton gloves are also helpful when handling the gilded item, until the surface has been properly sealed.

How to apply a metal-leaf finish

MATERIALS

FOR ALL METAL-LEAF FINISHES

- Acrylic or latex paint in desired color, for base coat; sponge applicator or paintbrush.
- 400-grit wet/dry sandpaper; damp cloth.
- Water-based gold-leaf adhesive size; sponge applicator or soft-bristled paintbrush.
- Composition gold or silver leaf, or pure copper leaf; scissors; thin cotton gloves, optional.
- Soft paintbrush, 1" (2.5 cm) wide, for tamping and smoothing metal leaf.
- Clear finish or aerosol clear acrylic sealer.

1. Apply thin coat of paint in the desired base-coat color over primed and sanded (page 12) surface, using sponge applicator; allow to dry. Repeat two or three times until painted surface is fully opaque.

2. Sand surface smooth, using 400-grit wet/dry sandpaper; wipe with damp cloth.

3. Apply light, even coat of size, using sponge applicator or brush; allow to set until clear, or about 30 minutes; surface will be tacky but not wet.

4. Cut the binding from book of metal leaf, using scissors. Remove two or three layers of metal leaf with supplied tissues at top and bottom; cut into quarters.

5. Hold piece of leaf between supplied tissues; avoid touching it directly with fingers. Slide bottom tissue from underneath leaf. Touching top tissue, press leaf in place over sized surface.

6

6. Remove top tissue. Using soft, dry paint-brush in an up-and-down motion, gently tamp the leaf in place to affix it. Then smooth leaf, using gentle stroking motion.

7. Apply additional pieces of leaf, overlapping them slightly, until the entire area is covered.

8. Brush over the surface of leaf in circular strokes, removing skewings of excess leaf at overlapped edges; reserve the skewings. Fill in any gaps by loading the brush with skewings and tamping in place. Reapply size to any gaps that will not hold skewings, using small brush. Allow to set; reapply skewings.

7

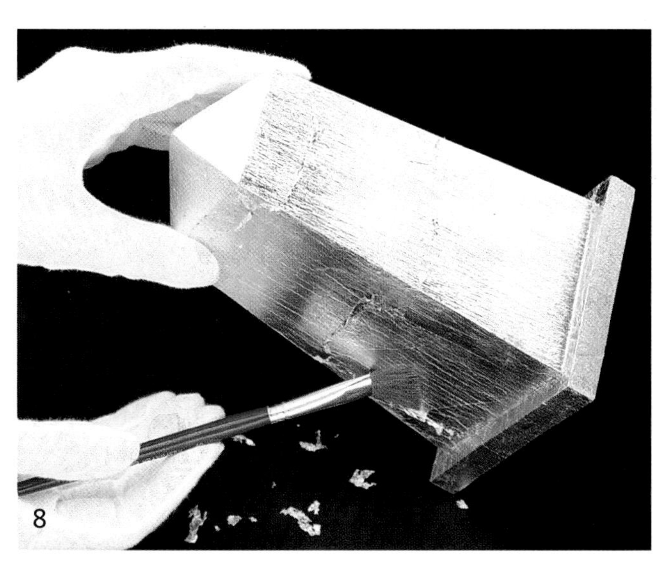

8

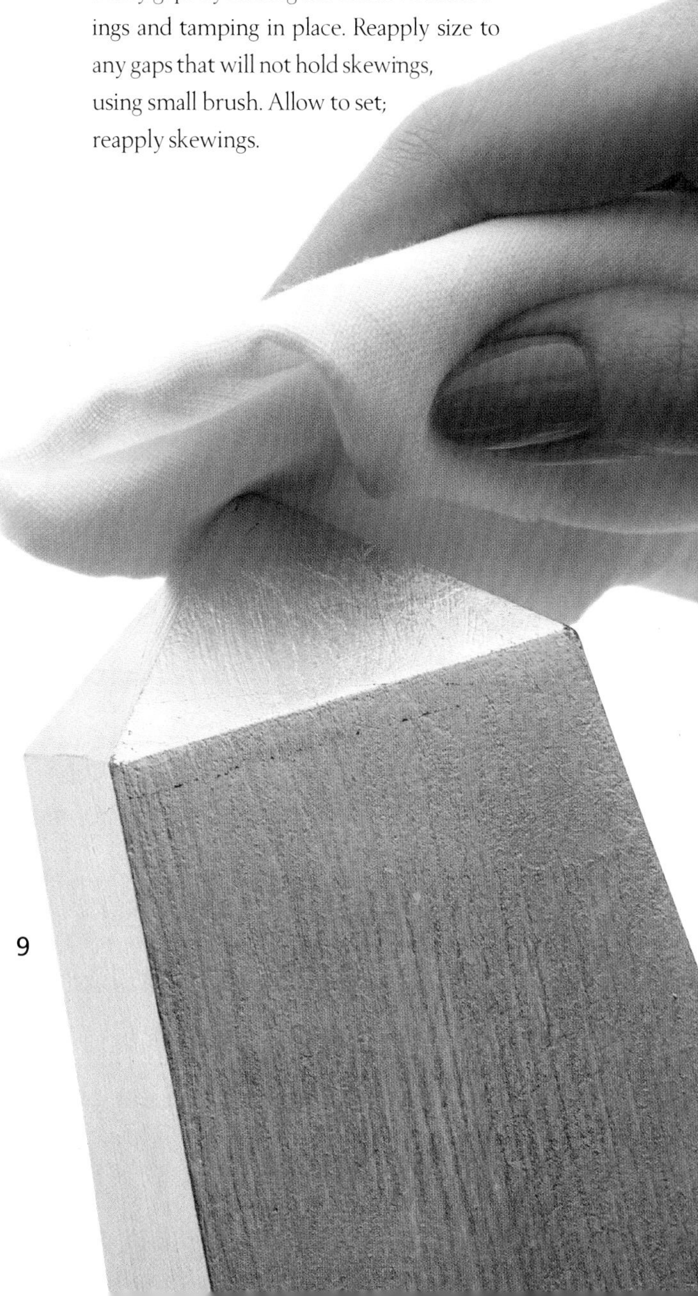

9

9. Buff the entire surface gently, using soft cotton cloth. Apply two thin coats of clear finish or aerosol clear acrylic sealer to prevent marring and tarnishing.

How to make a stencil for a metal-leaf design

MATERIALS

- Painter's masking tape.
- Sheet of glass; mat knife.
- Precut stencil or design and transfer paper.
- Basic materials for metal leafing (page 46).

1. Affix painter's masking tape to sheet of glass, covering area large enough to accommodate the entire design; overlap strips as needed. Transfer design onto taped surface, using carbon or graphite paper. Or trace design areas of the precut stencil onto taped surface with pencil.

2. Cut out design areas, using mat knife. Remove stencil carefully from glass.

How to apply metal leaf in isolated areas

1. Prepare the surface, as in steps 1 and 2 on page 46. Mask off desired area, using painter's masking tape (A), or affix prepared stencil to surface (B). Press tape firmly in place, making sure all cut edges are secured.

2. Apply light, even coat of size to areas that will be leafed in first color, using small paintbrush; size may extend onto the tape, but avoid areas that will be leafed in a different color. Allow to set until clear, or about 30 minutes; surface will be tacky but not wet.

3. Apply leaf to sized areas, following steps 4 to 6 on pages 46 and 47. Remove skewings and touch up gaps as in step 8 on page 47.

4. Repeat steps 2 and 3 for each additional metal-leaf color in design. Score metal leaf along edges of tape, using mat knife. Remove tape carefully. Apply clear finish or aerosol clear acrylic sealer to entire area.

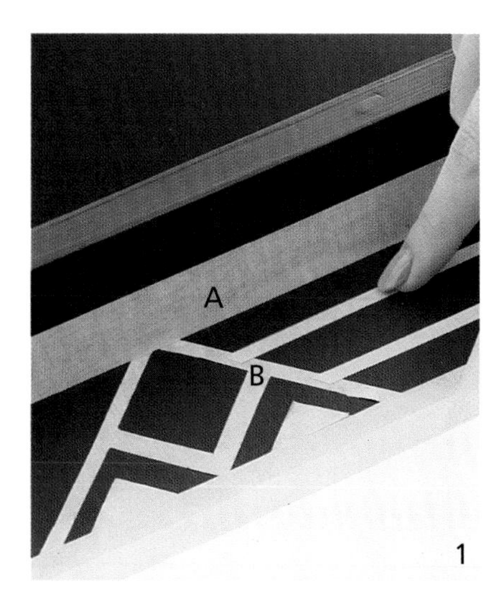

How to antique a metal-leafed surface

MATERIALS

- Basic materials for metal leafing.
- Antiquing solution, such as Modern Options' Patina Green™ or Patina Blue™, for antiquing pure copper leaf or composition gold leaf.
- Tinting solutions, such as Modern Options' Burgundy Tint™ and Black Tint™, for applying antiqued finish over composition silver leaf.
- Spray bottle for applying antiquing solution; applicator, such as sponge or cloth, for applying tinting solutions; toothbrush.
- Wet cloth.

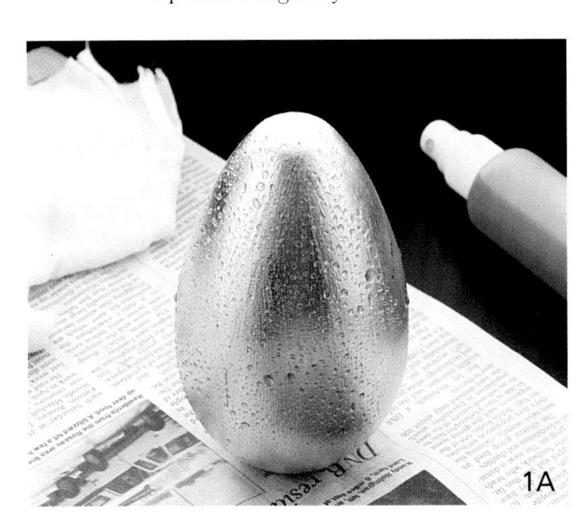

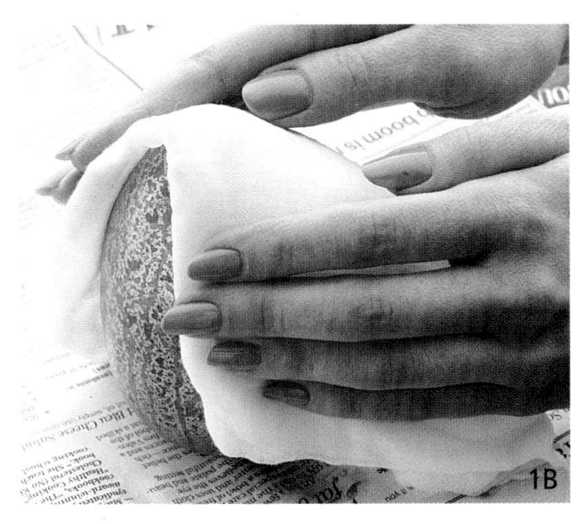

1A. PURE COPPER OR COMPOSITION GOLD LEAF. Apply leaf as in steps 1 to 8 on pages 46 and 47. Have a wet cloth near at hand. Apply antiquing solution to surface in fine mist, using spray bottle.

1B. Watch carefully as the solution reacts with metal leaf. When desired effect is reached (this happens quickly), cover surface with wet cloth to neutralize solution; blot the entire surface gently to remove solution. Allow to dry completely. Apply two thin coats of aerosol clear acrylic sealer.

2A. COMPOSITION SILVER LEAF. Apply leaf as in steps 1 to 8 on pages 46 and 47. Pour small amounts of tinting solutions into separate bowls. Dab solutions lightly onto surface, using desired applicators; blend solutions on surface to achieve desired effect. Allow to dry.

2B. Speck the surface lightly, using black tinting solution and toothbrush. Allow to dry. Apply two thin coats of aerosol clear acrylic sealer.

Gold-leaf Finish with an Aged Look

A gold-leaf finish with an aged look gives found objects with intricate carved or raised detailing a rich, old-world effect. With its timeless, mellow look, this finish is often used for the picture frames of fine artwork found in museums. Because it may be used on wood, plaster, or cast-resin furnishings, it is also suitable for sconces, candlesticks, and small pieces of furniture. Although the finish requires several steps, the process is easy and the results are exquisite.

For this finish, use imitation gold leaf, sold in craft and art stores. For the dimensional effect, various materials are used in addition to the gold leaf, creating layers and depth. First, a base coat of paint is applied. Then the gold leaf is applied, followed by a clear acrylic sealer that protects the gold leaf from tarnishing. Because the gold leaf is almost translucent, the color of the base coat contributes to the color of the gold leaf. A red base coat, for example, gives a warm, rich gold finish, while a white or gold base coat results in a lighter, brighter finish.

The remaining steps are designed to give the worn, old-world look to the finish. A heavy coat of latex or acrylic paint in taupe or cream is applied, then wiped away before it dries, except in the crevices and recessed areas. This is followed by a dusting of rottenstone powder, available at hardware stores, to add texture and aging to the gold-leaf finish.

MATERIALS

- Imitation gold leaf; water-based gold-leaf adhesive.
- Latex or acrylic paint in red or gold, for the base coat.
- Latex or acrylic paint in taupe, beige, or cream, for the top coat.
- Polyvinyl acrylic primer, if item is plaster.
- Rottenstone powder.
- Aerosol clear acrylic sealer.
- Paintbrushes, for applying paint, gold-leaf adhesive, and rottenstone powder; clean, lint-free rags; terry-cloth towel.
- 100-grit sandpaper, black paint, for a simplified method.

How to apply a gold-leaf finish with an aged look

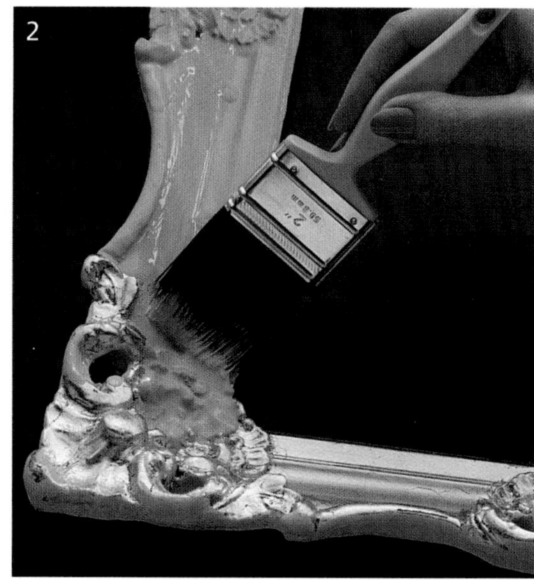

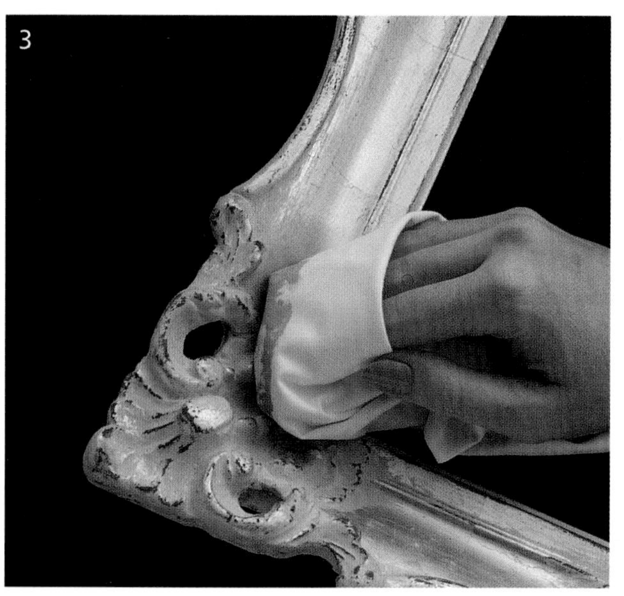

1. Clean the found object as necessary. Apply gold leaf as in steps 1 to 8 on pages 46 and 47. Apply two coats of aerosol clear acrylic sealer; allow to dry.

2. Apply a heavy coat of latex or acrylic paint in a taupe, beige, or cream, over the gold leafing. On a large project, work on one section at a time, applying the paint and completing step 3 before moving on to the next section.

3. Allow paint to partially dry; when paint begins to set, wipe paint off with a clean, lint-free rag. Start by applying light pressure, and then rubbing harder, if necessary. Remove most of the paint in the smooth areas, leaving paint in the carved areas, the crevices, and corners. If paint is difficult to remove, a slightly damp rag may be used.

4. Sprinkle a generous amount of rottenstone powder over the entire project while paint is still slightly damp. Tamp the powder down, using a paintbrush. Leave rottenstone powder on project for 20 minutes; then remove the excess powder with a soft-bristle paintbrush.

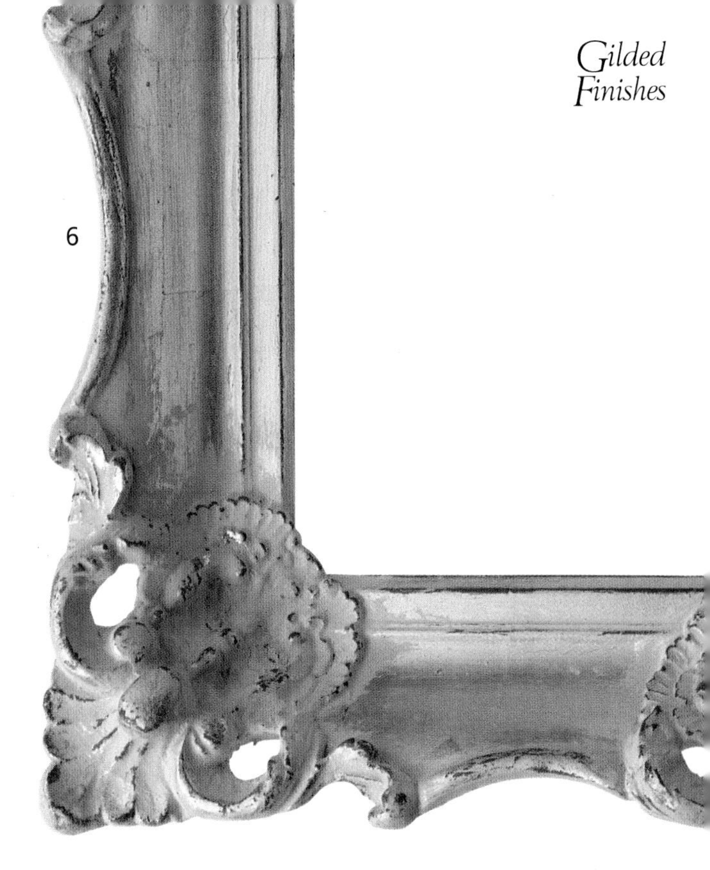

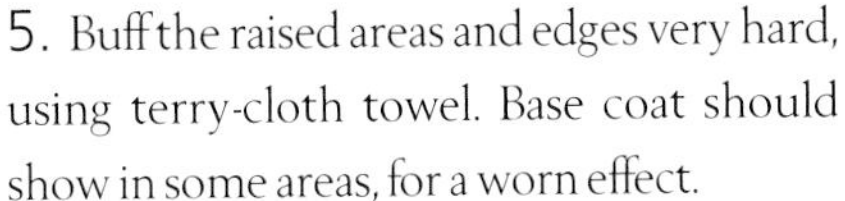

5. Buff the raised areas and edges very hard, using terry-cloth towel. Base coat should show in some areas, for a worn effect.

6. Buff and polish the smooth areas, using slightly damp rag; do not rub too hard, so gold leaf is not disturbed. Finished project appears worn in raised areas, corners, and edges where base coat peeks through, with the top coat of paint and the rottenstone in the recessed areas; the smooth areas are gold and shiny. Do not apply another coat of sealer, because it would cause the rottenstone to disintegrate.

1. SIMPLIFIED METHOD. Apply leaf as in steps 1 to 8 on pages 46 and 47. Allow gold leaf to set for 1 hour. Scratch the surface, using folded piece of 100-grit sandpaper; this allows the base coat to show in some areas. Wipe surface to remove any grit.

2. Speck project with black paint, testing the technique first. Dip the toothbrush into diluted black acrylic or flat latex paint; blot on paper towel. Run craft stick or finger along bristles of the toothbrush to spatter specks of paint onto the surface. Apply clear finish or aerosol clear acrylic sealer.

Gilded Designs

Create stunning guilded designs on the flat surfaces of furniture and accessories. In this technique, metallic powders are stenciled onto a surface of tacky varnish. The result is a stenciled design that is much smoother and more subtle than that achieved by stenciling with metallic paints.

Oil-based paint and varnish are used for this technique because the varnish remains tacky for a longer time. Metallic powders are available at art supply stores in a wide range of colors, from silvery white to rich bronze gold. Select an accessory or furniture item with smooth, flat surfaces, lightly sanding any prevarnished surfaces to ensure paint adhesion.

MATERIALS

- Oil-based paint for base coat.
- Oil-based clear varnish in gloss or semi-gloss finish.
- Metallic powder in desired color.
- Precut Mylar® stencil.
- Masking tape.
- Scrap of velvet or chamois leather.

How to apply a gilded design

1. Apply a base coat of oil-based paint to a clean, prepared surface; allow to dry. Apply a coat of varnish. Allow varnish to dry about 3 to 5 hours, until slightly tacky; at this time, if the corner of stencil is pressed against the varnish, stencil can be removed with a slight pull, but will leave no mark.

2. Pour a small amount of metallic powder into a bowl. Position the stencil in desired location; cover surrounding area on tray by taping paper to stencil.

3. Wrap a scrap of velvet or chamois leather around index finger, wrapping it smoothly so there are no wrinkles or creases at fingertip. Dip wrapped finger into the metallic powder; rub on a piece of paper to remove excess powder.

4. Gently rub area to be gilded, starting at the center and working out. As necessary, pick up more powder and reposition stencil. Remove stencil, and allow varnish to dry at least 24 hours.

5. Remove any powder outside design area by rubbing gently with mild abrasive cleanser. Wash the surface gently, using soapy water. Rinse and dry.

6. Seal the gilding by applying a coat of varnish; allow varnish to dry.

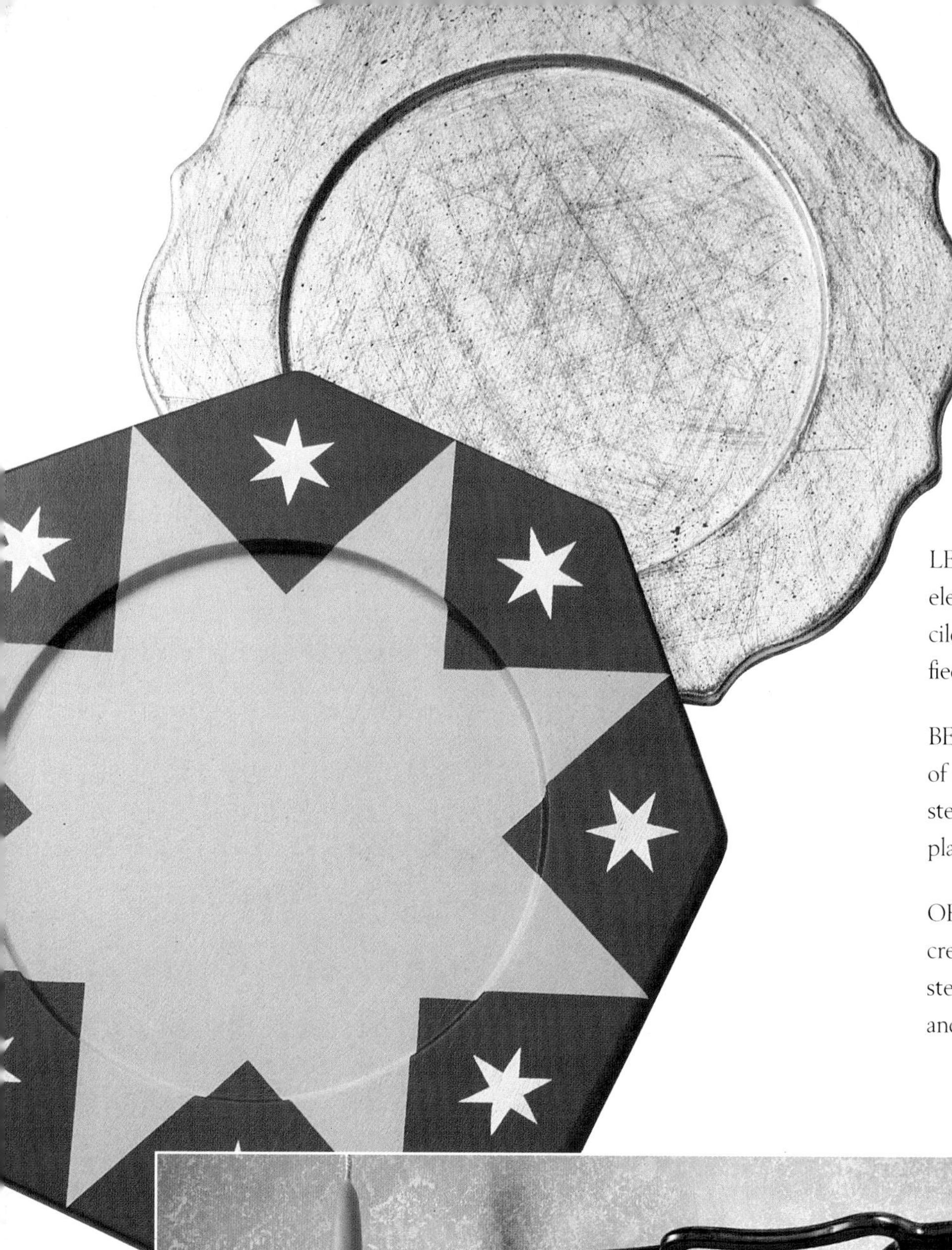

More ideas for gilding

LEFT: GOLD-LEAFED CHARGERS add elegance to the table setting. Apply stenciled gold-leaf designs (page 48) or a simplified antique finish (page 53).

BELOW: GILDED TRAY with two colors of metallic powder is achieved by using a stencil kit that contains a separate stencil plate for each metallic color.

OPPOSITE: GILDED ACCESSORIES are created using a variety of methods, including stenciling (urn), simple antiquing (bowl), and traditional gold leafing (candlestick).

Continued

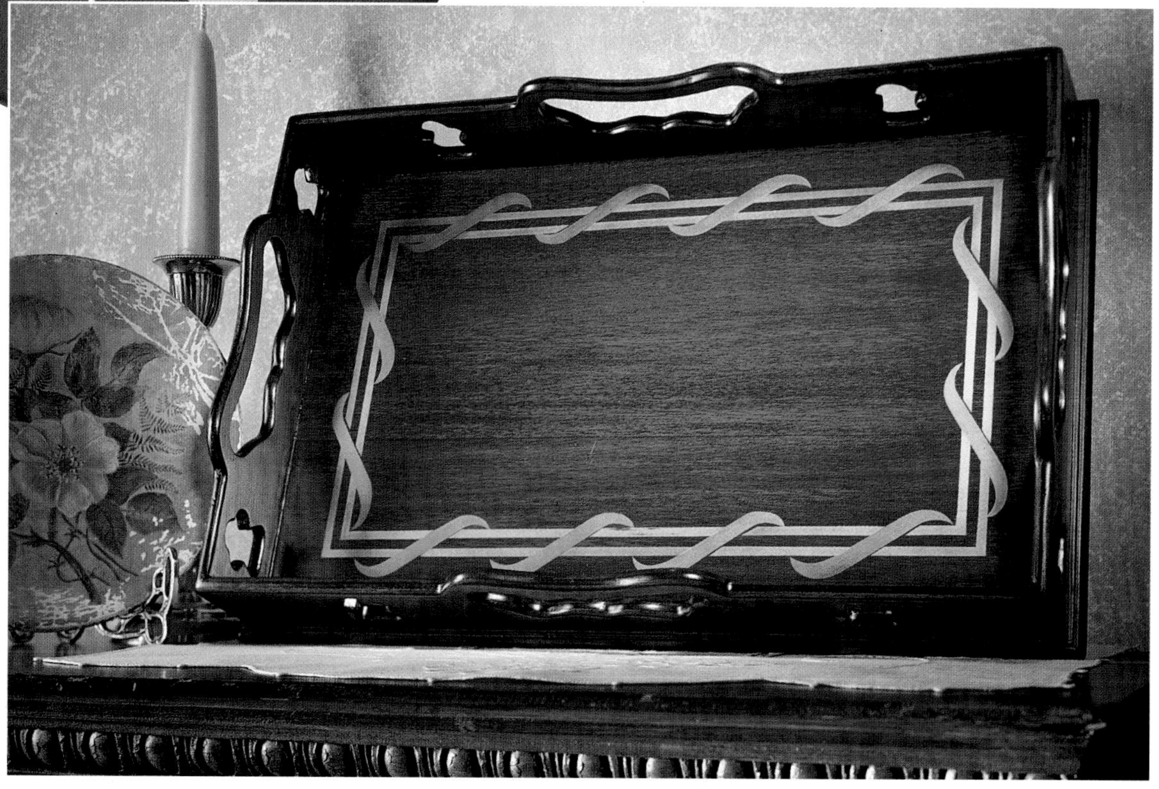

More ideas for gilding

(CONTINUED)

OPPOSITE AND BELOW: GOLD AND SILVER SKEWINGS tamped randomly over a sized surface leave a free-form metallic pattern, as in the center charger. The speckled copper-leaf finish on the platter and small plate is achieved by applying adhesive size lightly to the surface, using a sea sponge. Leaf adheres in the pattern left by the sponge.

LEFT: GOLD-LEAF WALL SHELVES with an antiqued finish (page 51) can display bud vases filled with fresh flowers, pieces of sculpture, or a favorite collection of accessories.

Index

CY DECOSSE INCORPORATED

President/COO: Nino Tarantino
Executive V.P./Editor-in-Chief: William B. Jones
Chairman Emeritus: Cy DeCosse

Creative Touches™
Group Executive Editor: Zoe A. Graul
Managing Editor: Elaine Johnson
Editor: Linda Neubauer
Associate Creative Director: Lisa Rosenthal
Senior Art Director: Delores Swanson
Art Director: Mark Jacobson
Copy Editor: Janice Cauley
Desktop Publishing Specialist: Laurie Kristensen
Sample Production Manager: Carol Olson
Photo Studio Services Manager: Marcia Chambers
Publishing Production Manager: Kim Gerber

President/COO: Philip L. Penny

METALLIC FINISHES ETC.
Created by: The Editors of Cy DeCosse Incorporated

Also available in the Creative Touches™ series:

Stenciling Etc., Sponging Etc., Stone Finishes Etc., Valances Etc., Painted Designs Etc., Swags Etc., Papering Projects Etc.

The Creative Touches™ series draws from the individual titles of The Home Decorating Institute®. Individual titles are also available from the publisher and in bookstores and fabric stores.

Printed on American paper by:
R. R. Donnelley & Sons Co.
99 98 97 96 / 5 4 3 2 1

Cy DeCosse Incorporated offers a variety of how-to books.

For information write:
Cy DeCosse Subscriber Books
5900 Green Oak Drive
Minnetonka, MN 55343